Using Leveled Books

Your Classroom Guide

Table of Contents

Introduction

Developing Strategic Readers

Using Leveled Texts Within Small-Group Reading Lessons

Introduction

Small-Group Reading Instruction Within a Comprehensive Literacy Program

Primary and intermediate school teachers have discovered the powerful effects of comprehensive literacy instruction that includes reading aloud, shared reading, small-group reading, independent reading, word study, writing, and ongoing assessment.

While observing and documenting each student's current strategies, the teacher will eventually find groups in which some students are developing at a faster or slower rate than the others, even though they started with similar strengths and needs. When this happens, the teacher should move the students to other groups based on evidence of their literacy learning. This type of dynamic, flexible grouping allows the teacher to individualize instruction rather than having static groups of learners follow the same prescribed paths.

In small-group reading, the emphasis is on practicing and extending a variety of competencies. These include:

- learning the academic content vocabulary integral to understanding the topic at hand
- making connections between the text and prior knowledge and experiences
- monitoring comprehension and using appropriate fix-up strategies, such as asking questions, visualizing, and rereading
- using text features, such as the table of contents, headings, glossary, index, bullets, sidebars, and captions, to locate information
- interpreting graphic features, such as diagrams, tables, charts, maps, and graphs
- using comprehension strategies, such as comparing and contrasting, drawing conclusions, and evaluating author's purpose
- decoding a wide array of visual patterns and word parts
- noting the author's grammar and usage, and understanding how they contribute to the reader's comprehension
- summarizing the key concepts in the text
- answering text-dependent questions about the text
- practicing techniques that improve reading fluency

Developing Strategic Readers

Essential Skills and the Reading Process

Current research identifies phonemic awareness, phonics, fluency, vocabulary, and comprehension as the five essential skills for reading success.

- **Phonemic awareness** is the ability to notice, think about, and work with the individual sounds in spoken words. Before children learn to read print, they need to become aware of how the sounds in words work. They must understand that words are made up of speech sounds, or phonemes.
- **Phonics** instruction teaches children the relationships between the letters (graphemes) of written language and the individual sounds (phonemes) of spoken language. Children learn to use the relationships to read and write words. Knowing the relationships will help children recognize familiar words accurately and automatically, and decode new words.
- **Fluency** is the ability to read a text accurately and quickly. When fluent readers read silently, they recognize words automatically. They group words quickly to help them gain meaning from what they read. Fluent readers read aloud effortlessly and with expression. Their reading sounds natural, as if they are speaking. Fluency is important because it provides a bridge between word recognition and comprehension. Because fluent readers do not have to concentrate on decoding the words, they can focus their attention on what the text means.
- **Vocabulary** refers to the words we must know to communicate effectively. Oral vocabulary refers to words that we use in our speech or recognize while listening to others speak. Reading vocabulary refers to words we recognize or use in print. Vocabulary plays an important part in learning to read. As beginning readers, children use the words they have heard to make sense of the words they see in print. Vocabulary also is very important to reading comprehension. Readers cannot understand what they are reading without knowing what most of the words mean.
- **Comprehension** is the reason for reading. If a student can read the words but does not understand what he is reading, he is not really reading. Good readers have a purpose for reading and think actively as they read. Research has shown that instruction in comprehension can help students understand, remember, and communicate with others about what they read.

(From "Put Reading First," based on the 2000 report of the National Reading Panel and published jointly by the National Institute for Literacy, the National Institute of Child Health and Human Development, and the U.S. Department of Education.)

Each of these skills can be addressed in a small-group setting using leveled texts at the students' instructional level. However, in order for learners to reach high levels of literacy development, teachers must also be knowledgeable about the reading process. They must be able to identify the strengths of their students and use this information to design appropriate literacy experiences that promote problem solving. The main goal of reading instruction is to create proficient readers who have a repertoire of strategies for independent reading. An important characteristic of a good reader is that he or she integrates the cueing system while reading fluently and expressively, focusing primarily on meaning.

The Cueing System

Cues are simply sources of information. A reader constantly builds and integrates these networks of information and uses them to check and confirm his or her responses to a text. The three sources of text information, or cues, are:

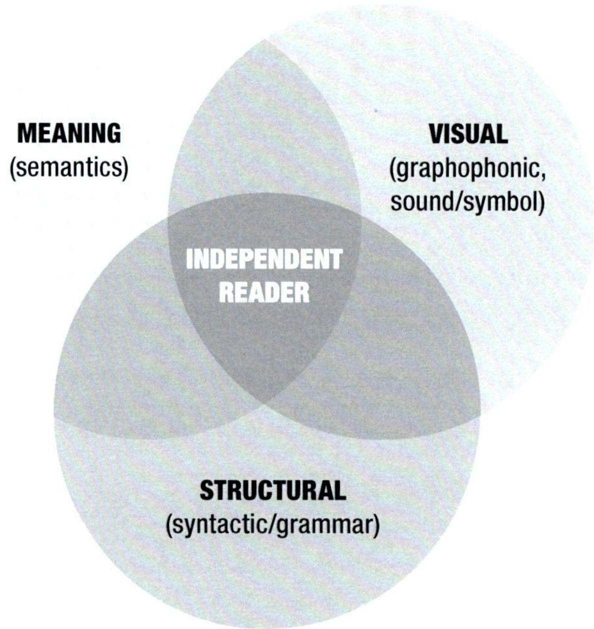

1. **Meaning Cues:** These relate to the author's intended message and purpose. They also involve the reader's background knowledge and identification of particular concepts found in the text. The pictures help the reader gain access to the meaning of the text as well.
2. **Structural Cues:** These are derived from the reader's oral language and exposure to book talk. Good readers monitor their grammatical substitutions by asking, "Does it sound right this way?"
3. **Visual Cues:** Graphophonics relates to the letters, words, and sounds that are incorporated in a text. These elements of the text require the reader to access the visual information in order to read the text.

Comprehension and Metacognition

Comprehension strategies are mental problem-solving actions initiated by a reader to gain meaning from the text. Metacognition, or "thinking about thinking," takes strategic reading one step further by helping us recognize how we process information. Effective readers use comprehension and metacognitive strategies in conjunction to develop a deeper understanding of a content-area topic, a character's motives, a book's theme, and the like. They construct knowledge through a variety of different venues and identify when they no longer understand and what they can do about it. Although we can't observe these mental behaviors, we see evidence that a student is employing the strategies of an efficient processing system as he or she exhibits some of the following behaviors.

Monitor-Reading Strategies

Good readers use monitor-reading strategies before, during, and after reading to monitor their comprehension and help them stay fully engaged in a text. Although good readers perform all these strategies on all types of reading, students will focus on one particular strategy in their daily reading.

Reading instruction begins with the teacher explaining what the strategy is and why it is important for readers to use. Then the teacher models her own use of the strategy by thinking aloud about a section of the text she has read with the students. After the modeling, the teacher guides students as they practice the strategy during further reading of the text. After reading, teacher and students reflect on how they used the strategy and how it helped them as readers. As students become more proficient throughout the week's instruction, they apply the strategy more and more independently. The ultimate goal of instruction is to ensure that students develop strategies they can transfer to new reading experiences.

Monitor-Reading Strategy	Explanation
Ask Questions	Readers often pause during reading to wonder about the text. They ask questions to help them understand and stay involved in what they are reading.
Determine Text Importance	Readers determine text importance when they identify big ideas, themes, and specific information when they read. They may also evaluate the author's purpose and point of view.
Make Connections	Readers make connections when they link what they read to something they already know. Readers make three types of connections to texts: text-to-self, text-to-text, text-to-world
Retell	Readers retell when they put ideas from a text into their own words. Retelling ensures that readers stop and reflect on the text.
Reread	Good readers reread text to clarify and refine their understanding of it. Even the most accomplished readers get confused from time to time and need to utilize this strategy.
Stop, Think, and Write	When monitoring comprehension, readers who use monitor-reading strategies resist the urge to read quickly through a text. They stop and think about what they've read. Students will produce written responses to questions that relate directly to the text. These responses will show evidence that the students understand the content. Writing about what was read allows students to reflect on the text and clarify their thoughts.

Comprehension Strategies

The teacher explains and models the strategy using a real-world example. Next, the teacher models using the strategy in the context of the content-area reading text. The teacher records this strategy information using a graphic organizer.

After the teacher has modeled, students practice using the strategy on another section of the text they have read. With the teacher's help, students add information to the comprehension strategy graphic organizer. Finally, students apply the strategy independently or with a partner by rereading another section of the text to complete the graphic organizer.

Comprehension Strategies	
Analyze Text Structure and Organization	Determine the text structure to better understand what the author is saying and to use as research when text must be analyzed.
Compare and Contrast	Find ways that two things are alike and different.
Draw Conclusions	Determine what the author is suggesting without directly stating it. Conclusions are made during and after reading, and are made from multiple (3+) pieces of information from the text. Students' conclusions will vary, but must be drawn from the evidence in the text and background knowledge.
Identify Cause and Effect	Find things that happened (effect) and why they happened (cause). Text may contain multiple causes and effects.
Identify Main Idea and Supporting Details	Determine what the paragraph, page, or chapter is mostly about. Sometimes the main idea is stated and sometimes it is implied. Students must choose details that support the main idea, not "just any detail."
Identify Sequence of Events	Determine order of events for topics such as history, science, or biography.
Analyze Character	Use clues about a character to tell what that character is like or what he/she might do.
Make Inferences	Determine what the author is suggesting without directly stating it. Inferences are usually made during reading and are made from one or two pieces of information from the text. Students' inferences will vary but must be made from the evidence in the text and background knowledge.
Make Predictions	Determine what might happen next in a story or nonfiction piece. Predictions are based on information presented in the text.
Summarize Information	Take key ideas from the text and put them together to create a shorter version of the original text. Summaries should have few, if any, details.

The Reading/Writing Connection

The collection and analysis of independent writing samples provides teachers with valuable information about how students process literacy information, and supports teachers' decisions concerning reading instruction. For example, consider how the following goals for beginning writers correspond to goals for beginning readers.

- Generate a complete thought
- Know where to start writing
- Follow directional movement
- Make a one-to-one voice-to-print match
- Understand the concepts of letters, words, and punctuation
- Reread to predict and confirm
- Demonstrate knowledge of letter formations
- Articulate slowly and record sounds in words
- Demonstrate knowledge of a growing store of high-frequency words

As students grow as writers and begin to compose longer pieces of text, teachers evaluate and support the following literacy behaviors.

- Composing text using various genres
- Composing text according to purpose and audience
- Conforming to expository text structures in informational writing, such as description, problem/solution, sequential/time order, compare/contrast, cause/effect, procedural, and narrative
- Writing independently for self and others
- Incorporating descriptive language
- Gathering information on a topic, sorting it into categories, and using categories to write paragraphs
- Using graphic organizers to plan
- Revising for content and clarity
- Editing for spelling and correct use of capitalization, punctuation, and proper nouns
- Editing for standard grammar usage and subject/verb agreement
- Developing a writer's "voice"
- Using resources, such as a dictionary, thesaurus, and spell-check
- Applying knowledge of the writer's craft from texts read to original writing

Assessment

Assessment and evaluation are an integral part of the daily routine in a literacy curriculum. The comprehensive literacy philosophy views teaching as a process of making instructional decisions based on observations of the students' strengths and needs. Thoughtful assessment provides teachers with essential knowledge about what students know and how they think. Although formal pretests and posttests are vital for documentation and planning purposes, systematic observation is the heart of the evaluation process. Observations need to be ongoing and multifaceted and must occur in authentic contexts. Assessment components that students can create and maintain include:

- Reading and writing surveys and interviews
- Reading and writing logs and reflections
- Writing samples and reflections
- Writing assessment frames

Assessment components that teachers can administer and maintain include:

- Anecdotal notes
- Oral reading record analysis forms
- Retelling rubrics, both oral and written
- Text-level progress charts for small-group reading
- Reading and writing observation checklists
- Anecdotal records
- Specific comprehension skill evaluations
- Comprehensive pretests and posttests

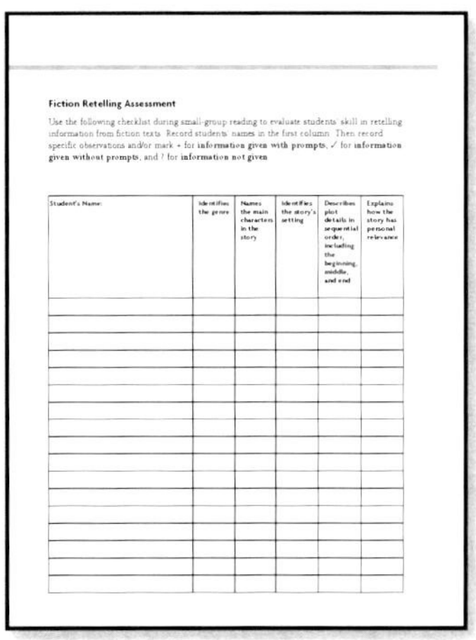

Fiction Retelling Assessment

Use the following checklist during small-group reading to evaluate students' skill in retelling information from fiction texts. Record students' names in the first column. Then record specific observations and/or mark + for **information given with prompts**, ✓ for **information given without prompts**, and ? for **information not given**.

Student's Name:	Identifies the genre	Names the main characters in the story	Identifies the story's setting	Describes plot details in sequential order, including the beginning, middle, and end	Explains how the story has personal relevance

Fiction Retelling Assessment

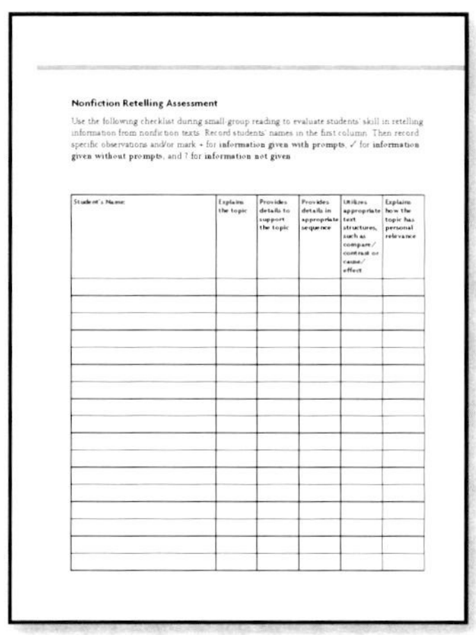

Nonfiction Retelling Assessment

Use the following checklist during small-group reading to evaluate students' skill in retelling information from nonfiction texts. Record students' names in the first column. Then record specific observations and/or mark + for **information given with prompts**, ✓ for **information given without prompts**, and ? for **information not given**.

Student's Name:	Explains the topic	Provides details to support the topic	Provides details in appropriate sequence	Utilizes appropriate text structures, such as compare/contrast or cause/effect	Explains how the topic has personal relevance

Nonfiction Retelling Assessment

Using Leveled Texts Within Small-Group Reading Lessons

When Are Students Ready for Small-Group Reading Instruction?

Observations play a critical role in deciding what type of support students need. To determine if young students are ready to participate in a formal small-group setting, the teacher carefully observes them during whole-group and individual endeavors, such as shared reading, independent or buddy reading, interactive writing, and journal writing.

During these literacy events, the teacher collects information on how children respond to print and interact with text, noting answers to the following questions.

During Reading

- Are students aware of early reading behaviors such as directionality and one-to-one matching?
- Can they distinguish letters from words?
- Can they locate a few high-frequency words in the text, such as *I, a,* or *the*?
- Do they join in during the shared-reading experience and predict language structures?
- Can they construct meaning using the pictures as a guide?

During Writing

- Do students use letter forms when they write?
- Do they link some sounds with symbols when they write?
- Do they articulate words slowly as they write?

If the answer to some of the questions is "yes," the teacher can begin to group the students according to established needs. However, some students may need many more opportunities and experiences with print before taking an active part during the first reading of the leveled text, while others are ready to move on to more complex strategies. The teacher's knowledge of the reading process is key.

(From *Apprenticeship in Literacy: Transitions Across Reading and Writing* by Linda Dorn, Cathy French, and Tammy Jones. Stenhouse, 1999.)

Characteristics of Readers

Following are some of the significant behaviors to observe and support in students reading at different developmental reading levels.

Emergent Grades K–1 Levels: A–C (1–4) D–E (5–8)	• Nonfiction/Fiction • 16 pages; print on only 8 of the pages • Direct-to-high picture/text match • Developmental print placement • High-frequency word at the beginning of every line for return sweep • Predictable language patterns • Structural changes
Early Grade 1 Levels: F–G (9–12) H–I (13–16)	• Nonfiction/Fiction • 16 pages • Moderate-to-low picture/text match • High-frequency word at the beginning of every line for fluency

Readers at Levels A–C/1–4

- Reads fluently; problem solves on one or two things only
- Uses one-to-one matching
- Uses directionality
- Uses return sweep
- Knows a small core of high-frequency words that can be read fluently
- Rereads independently to confirm or disconfirm predictions
- Rereads by returning to the beginning of the sentence
- Rereads at the point of difficulty and articulates the first letter of the problem word
- Checks predictions at the point of difficulty with the picture (cross-checking)

Readers at Levels D–E/5–8

- Returns to reread closer to the point of difficulty
- Begins to search through a difficult word for additional information
- Uses beginning chunks, or parts of words, and ending sounds fluently
- Uses meaning and structure to guide reading
- Integrates meaning, structure, and visual cues, moving toward automaticity

Grouping Students for Small-Group Instruction

The teacher's role is to take each student from her current level of literacy development and advance her to higher levels. Therefore, each student must be assessed in order for the teacher to know the strengths and weaknesses of each individual. Grouping students with like abilities makes sense for the teacher and makes teaching manageable.

A student's current level of literacy knowledge is the basis for grouping and planning instruction. Texts should be selected so that each member of the group can read with at least 90 percent accuracy. Students may also be grouped by:

- Comprehension strategy
- Developmental literacy characteristics
- Monitor-reading strategies such as analyzing a new word, rereading, etc.
- Concepts about print
- Language structures
- Ability to decode
- Known high-frequency words
- Knowledge of text structures
- Genres
- Text levels
- Topic of interest

Because students' needs are changing, it is imperative for teachers to use ongoing observations and assessments to plan small-group instruction. Grouping should be dynamic. By grouping in different ways for different purposes, the teacher can avoid the stigma of labeling students as struggling readers. Students also learn to interact cooperatively with the other members of the class in a small-group setting.

Use the Characteristics of Readers found on page 10 of this guide to group students according to developmental characteristics by level of text. Also, be sure to use the grouping forms and the other Fidelity of Implementation Forms found in the Appendix of this guide.

One thing to remember when grouping students is that a book is too difficult for a student if he cannot read it with at least 90 percent accuracy. Also, check to make sure that the student is reading strategically.

On the other end of the spectrum, if a student reads a text fluently with no problem-solving actions, then the book is most likely at a level that is too easy to be used in a small-group setting with the support of the teacher. The student should be reading at a higher level. However, the student may read that text independently for fluency practice.

Selecting Texts to Match the Needs of Readers

Prior to a small-group reading session, teachers select leveled texts that they feel the students can read successfully, with an accuracy rate of 90 percent or better. Book selection plays a major role in assisting students' learning at optimum rates. Selections based on students' interests, prior knowledge, and competencies spur their development by building upon strengths. This dynamic process stems from ongoing observation and assessments, such as oral reading records and writing samples. To select appropriate leveled texts, teachers should consider:

- The text layout
- The book language
- The supportive and challenging features of the book
- Whether the concepts and vocabulary used in the book are meaningful to the students
- Whether the structural language patterns are within the students' control
- The students' oral language abilities
- The students' current strategies and competencies for problem solving at difficult points in a chosen text
- Whether the book promotes fluency

In order for a student to practice effective reading behaviors, a book should contain more supportive features than challenges. This places the focus on helping the student build a smoothly operating reading system, whereby reading improves with practice.

Teachers can select specific leveled texts to teach the skills and strategies outlined in the Comprehension and Metacognition section, along with word-solving skills, such as:

- Identifying synonyms, antonyms, and homonyms
- Using context clues to determine word meaning
- Using knowledge of word structures to determine word meaning
- Identifying multiple-meaning words
- Understanding denotation and connotation

In addition, teachers can select texts from a wide variety of fiction genres and nonfiction content areas.

Another way teachers can support students' literacy instruction is to select nonfiction leveled texts that exhibit the following carefully controlled text features and graphic aids.

Careful use of prepositions, tenses, and pronouns

Varied print placement and captions

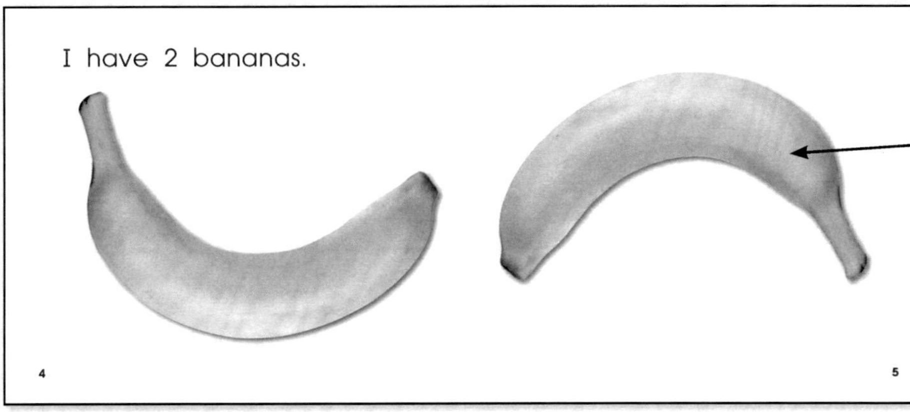

Direct photo/ picture support

The Small-Group Reading Lesson Sequence

Small-group reading is an assisted literacy experience in which the teacher supports and guides students with texts on their instructional level before, during, and after reading. Each small group consists of two to six students. The flexible setting allows the teacher to match students' reading abilities to appropriate materials, to observe reading behaviors, and to model and prompt for specific strategies that will improve students' word solving, comprehension, and fluency.

Before Reading

The small-group reading sequence begins by activating prior knowledge about the concepts, people, places, and objects that appear in the text that students will read. This is generally done before making direct reference to the book so that students approach the text already having connections to it.

The next crucial step is orienting students to the leveled text. Each member of the group is given his or her own copy. The students then locate the title and author, study the front cover illustration, and collaborate with the teacher in an introductory conversation about the book.

- For emergent to early students, the teacher provides a brief overview of the text and then prompts students to discuss the pictures and the author's intended message. The teacher incorporates structure by exposing the students to recurring language patterns and introduces visual or graphophonic cues by having students locate a known high-frequency word or predict the letter that they would expect to find at the beginning, middle, or end of a word.
- For fluent and advanced fluent students, the teacher provides a brief overview of the text and asks questions that prompt students to make predictions, such as: Will the book be fiction or nonfiction? What kinds of text features might be encountered in this text? What information might be presented? What might happen to the characters? What special vocabulary might the author use?

Both types of introductions prepare students to read the book by creating a supportive context for building meaning and providing an opportunity to discuss specific strategies that might be helpful during the reading, including using a related graphic organizer. The teacher then sets a purpose for the reading that may include a brief model of what the students' expectations will be during the first read.

Planning Before Reading

- *I'm going to read a nonfiction book, but I really don't know much about the topic. I think I should read slowly.*
- *I wonder why . . .*
- *I already know _____ about this topic.*
- *I've skimmed through the book. I know the word _____, but I don't know what _____ means.*
- *I saw _____ before when I went to . . .*
- *I skimmed through the book and saw lots of graphics and charts. I'll need to use those to help me understand what I'm about to read.*
- *I see some clue words or phrases that might help me figure out the text structure of this book.*

During Reading

Students whisper-read or read silently, depending on their developmental level, as the teacher observes and monitors. To keep interruptions to a minimum, the teacher only intervenes when a student appears to be in jeopardy of losing the meaning of the text. The teacher then uses language prompts to help the student apply a specific problem-solving strategy at the point of difficulty.

Fluent and intermediate students may use self-stick notes to flag sections of the text that support their ideas about the author's purpose, mark unfamiliar words or confusions, or note information for the graphic organizer.

Monitoring During Reading

- *When the author describes _____, I can picture it in my mind.*
- *I think _____ might happen next, because . . .*
- *This page was about . . .*
- *I need to remember _____ because it seems like an important point.*
- *Maybe I should reread this part and look for specific information.*
- *The graph (or other nonfiction text feature) on this page helps me understand . . .*
- *Since I don't understand this word, I may need to . . .*
- *This surprised me. I expected _____ because . . .*
- *Before I continue reading, I need to stop and think about what I just read and make sure I understand it. If I still don't understand, I need to make a plan.*

After Reading

A short book may be read all the way through, while a longer book may be divided among two or more days. Students should be asked to reflect on the reading—both their use of specific strategies and their understanding of the content. Next, the teacher revisits the selection with one or two important teaching points that extend the students' learning to a higher level. These points are based on careful observations of the students' processing behaviors during the reading. The teacher uses the opportunity to validate successful techniques, activate strategies the students neglected or those with which they experienced difficulty, and focus on specific words, text or graphic features, literary elements, or other important components. Finally, the teacher builds comprehension by:

- Having students retell all or parts of the text
- Helping students make personal connections to the information or story
- Asking concept and text-dependent questions and discussing students' responses
- Helping students complete their graphic organizers
- Working with students to synthesize and assess the reading selection

Over the next few days, students are encouraged to reread all or parts of the text to strengthen the newly made connections, foster cognitive development, and promote fluency. In addition, the teacher uses the familiar text for additional mini-lessons, writing activities, and content connections.

Evaluating After Reading

- *The strategies that worked well for me were . . .*
- *Next time, I think I'll . . .*
- *The strategies that didn't work for me were . . .*
- *I need to get help with . . .*

Teachers can use specific prompts to help students learn to integrate cues, check one source of information against another, and gain important feedback from the text. For example:

- *You said _____. Does that make sense?*
- *What word would make sense here?*
- *Look at the picture. What is happening?*
- *Does _____ sound right?*
- *Does _____ look right?*
- *Look at the first letter. Get your mouth ready to say it.*
- *It could be _____, but look at _____. Check to make sure what you read looks right and makes sense.*
- *Do you know something about the word that can help you?*
- *_____ makes sense, but look at the first letter.*
- *Try that again.*
- *What can you do to help yourself there?*
- *How would you start the word if you were writing it?*
- *Say the word slowly. What sounds can you hear?*
- *You went back and fixed the tricky part, didn't you? Good checking!*
- *You used a word you know to help you with this new word. That's what good readers do.*
- *Are you right?*
- *Go back and read that again.*
- *What did you notice?*
- *What else can you do?*
- *Read it again and see if you can find out what is wrong here.*
- *What can you do to help yourself?*
- *What is the book about?*
- *Do you know something about that word that can help you?*
- *What sound do you hear in the word _____? Say it slowly.*
- *Do you see a word on this page that has those letters?*

Scheduling Small-Group Reading Instruction

Leveled texts can be implemented in all tiers of a Response to Intervention (RTI) model through the use of flexible, small-group reading lessons.

- **Tier I:** small-group differentiated instruction in the daily core reading block
- **Tier II:** targeted small-group intervention lessons for at-risk students
- **Tier III:** intensive intervention lessons for high-risk students combined with explicit skills-focused lessons

As a teacher, it is important to set priorities in order of students' needs for implementation of small-group reading. Below you will find expectations for implementation according to students' proficiency levels.

Small-Group Reading Expectations

Students' Proficiency Levels	Expectations for Implementation
Exceeding grade-level expectations; above-level students	1–2 small-group reading lessons per week (Tier I)
Meeting grade-level expectations; on-level students	2–3 small-group reading lessons per week (Tier I)

Small-group reading lessons should last 20–30 minutes per day per group. Classroom teachers should be meeting with 2–4 small groups per day. Students with the greatest needs should be met with daily, with no less than three small-group lessons per week. Use the following chart to determine the proficiency levels of your students with beginning and end-of-year text-level progress expectations.

Progress Expectations

Grade Level	Beginning-of-Year Text Level	End-of-Year Text Level
Kindergarten	A/1	C/4
Grade 1	D/5	I/16
Grade 2	J/18	M/28
Grade 3	N/30	P/38
Grade 4	Q/40	R/40
Grade 5	S/44	U/50

Scheduling Options for Tier I Small-Group Guided Reading Lessons

Small-group guided reading lessons can be used by regular classroom teachers in order to differentiate instruction in Tier I and/or provide additional intervention lessons for Tiers II and III instruction.

The following is a sample schedule for an emergent or early classroom that shows one way to schedule small-group reading into the day.

8:00 A.M.	Read-Aloud and Shared Reading
8:30 A.M.	Letter and Word Study
9:00 A.M.	Small-Group Reading/Literacy Centers
9:45 A.M.	Recess
10:00 A.M.	Assisted Writing/Literacy Centers
10:30 A.M.	Journal Writing
10:45 A.M.	Handwriting
11:00 A.M.	Lunch/Recess/Additional Read-Aloud
12:00 A.M.	Content Connections (Integration of Social Studies, Math, and Science)
1:00 A.M.	Math
2:00 A.M.	Specials (Library, Music, Art, and Physical Education)
2:45 A.M.	Summary of Day
3:00 A.M.	Dismissal

It is critical to have at least two and a half hours of instructional time for the comprehensive literacy components of reading aloud, shared reading, small-group reading, independent reading, and writing. This suggested framework follows an apprenticeship approach because it includes explicit teaching interactions as well as opportunities for students to use their knowledge and to practice their strategies on independent tasks. Each teacher must adjust the sample schedule according to the time constraints of the instructional day. However, the specific components must remain to provide a comprehensive literacy curriculum and to create transitions in students' development.

What Are the Other Students Doing During Small-Group Instruction?

As we have seen, teachers need a block of uninterrupted time to meet with a small group, and the other students need to be engaged in activities that provide them with opportunities to extend their literacy knowledge. Students must also know what to do if they need help while the teacher is working with others and what to do if they finish their current tasks. The following list suggests activities that allow students to apply and practice reading and writing at an independent level.

- Reread a selection of familiar leveled texts alone or with a partner.
- Read posters, charts, and student-created texts that are displayed in the classroom.
- Listen to books on tape.
- Record information in reading logs or response journals.
- Record new words or words with certain phonetic elements in a personal dictionary.
- Locate literary devices such as similes, metaphors, and figurative language in texts.
- Compose or rebuild texts with sentence strips in a pocket chart.
- Engage in letter or word sorts.
- Write in journals.
- Write to pen pals.
- Work in Math, Science, and Social Studies centers.
- Work on research projects or reports.
- Participate in book studies or literature circles.

It is vital to establish a well-organized learning environment that provides a framework for familiar routines to promote students' independence. At the beginning of the year, the teacher may have all the students do the same activity.

As more activities are introduced, the teacher may appoint students to various activities or let them choose, depending on classroom organization, management, and teaching style.

Remember that it can take four to six weeks at the beginning of the school year for students to learn to work independently. Prepare them by:

1. Establishing appropriate behaviors
2. Modeling activities and establishing criteria for quality work
3. Allowing time for students to practice activities with your guidance before expecting them to proceed independently

Weekly Small-Group Reading Lesson Documentation Form

Appendix

Weekly Small-Group Reading Lesson Documentation Form

Teacher Name: ________ **School Name:** ________ **Grade Level:** ________

Week of: ________

Tier of Instruction:
- Tier I: 4–6 students
- Tier II: 3–5 students
- Tier III: 1–3 students

Student Names:

	Lesson Date: **Start/End Time:**	**Lesson Date:** **Start/End Time:**	**Lesson Date:** **Start/End Time:**	**Lesson Date:** **Start/End Time:**	**Lesson Date:** **Start/End Time:**
Book Title					
Book Level					
Lesson Instructional Focus					
Lesson Observations/ Notes					
Lesson Follow-Up/ Teaching Points					
Needs to Address in Next Lesson					
Other Comments/ Notes					

Weekly Small-Group Reading Lesson Grouping Form

Weekly Small-Group Reading Lesson Grouping Form

Teacher Name: ________ **School Name:** ________ **Grade Level:** ________

Week of: ________

Tier of Instruction:
- Tier I: 4–6 students
- Tier II: 3–5 students
- Tier III: 1–3 students

Small Group #1

Students' Names	Instructional Reading Level (90–94%)	Independent Reading Level (95–100%)	Proficiency Level: - Above Grade Level/Advanced - On Grade Level/Benchmark - Below Grade Level/ At Risk, Strategic - Far Below Grade Level/ High Risk, Intensive

Small Group #2

Students' Names	Instructional Reading Level (90–94%)	Independent Reading Level (95–100%)	Proficiency Level: - Above Grade Level/Advanced - On Grade Level/Benchmark - Below Grade Level/ At Risk, Strategic - Far Below Grade Level/ High Risk, Intensive

Small-Group Guided Reading Observation Record Levels 1–4

Small-Group Guided Reading Observation Record • Levels 1–4

Date: ______________________

Text Title: ______________________

Text Level: ______________________

Chart Coding Legend:
✓ reading behavior observed during lesson

Student's Name:	Reads fluently; problem-solves on one or two things only	One-to-one matching	Directionality	Return sweep	Knows a small core of high-frequency words that can be read fluently	Self-monitors and attends to print, using high-frequency words	Aware of errors and searches the picture as well as the print	Rereads by returning to the beginning of the sentence	Cross-checks prediction at point of difficulty with the picture and print	Rereads at point of difficulty and articulates the first letter of the problem word

Comments/Concerns:

Small-Group Guided Reading Observation Record Levels 5–8

Small-Group Guided Reading Observation Record • Levels 5–8

Date: ______________________

Text Title: ______________________

Text Level: ______________________

Chart Coding Legend:
✓ reading behavior observed during lesson

Student's Name:	Reads fluently; problem-solves on one or two things only	Returns to reread closer to the point of difficulty	Beginning to search through a difficult word for additional information by blending letters into sounds	Fluently uses beginning chunks, or parts of words, and ending sounds	Meaning and structure are guiding the reading	Integrating meaning, structure, and visual cues; is moving toward automaticity	Self-monitoring, or checking on himself or herself, moving toward automaticity	Analyzes words using graphophonic patterns	Reads high-frequency words fluently	Recognizes errors when reading and initiates problem-solving actions

Comments/Concerns:

Small-Group Guided Reading Observation Record Levels 9–16

Small-Group Guided Reading Observation Record • Levels 9–16

Date: ______________________

Text Title: ______________________

Text Level: ______________________

Chart Coding Legend:
✓ reading behavior observed during lesson

	Reads fluently; problem-solves on one or two things only	Problem-solves at the point of error and makes multiple attempts to self-correct	Searches through the difficult word and blends sounds together	Takes words apart using large units or syllables	Meaning and structure guide the reading; uses visual information to check on reading	Reads longer texts with greater accuracy	Uses word meaning and context clues to problem-solve	Increasing control of visual patterns and flexible use of strategies	Reads high-frequency words fluently

Comments/Concerns: ______________________

Nonfiction Retelling Assessment

Nonfiction Retelling Assessment

Use the following checklist during small-group reading to evaluate students' skill in retelling information from nonfiction texts. Record students' names in the first column. Then record specific observations and/or mark + for **information given with prompts**, ✓ for **information given without prompts**, and ? for **information not given**.

Student's Name:	Explains the topic	Provides details to support the topic	Provides details in appropriate sequence	Utilizes appropriate text structures, such as compare/contrast or cause/effect	Explains how the topic has personal relevance

Fiction Retelling Assessment

Fiction Retelling Assessment

Use the following checklist during small-group reading to evaluate students' skill in retelling information from fiction texts. Record students' names in the first column. Then record specific observations and/or mark **+** for **information given with prompts**, **✓** for **information given without prompts**, and **?** for **information not given**.

Student's Name:	Identifies the genre	Names the main characters in the story	Identifies the story's setting	Describes plot details in sequential order, including the beginning, middle, and end	Explains how the story has personal relevance

Glossary of Terms

anecdotal records: informal notes containing valuable information regarding students' strengths, weaknesses, progress, needs, and processing abilities

authentic assessment: the collection of written data taken as a student is observed at a specific moment in time; the data or examples taken from routinely practiced approaches in the actual settings in which students are normally engaged

caption: a statement placed under a photograph to extend the learner's knowledge of the content information

challenging text features: the aspects of the text that present a difficulty as a student reads, depending on his or her developmental level

classroom management: a teacher's ability to organize the instructional approaches of comprehensive literacy within the framework of the school day

coaching: giving hints, prompts, or reminders using explicit language to guide students

comprehensive literacy: a balance of instructional approaches, structural settings, and assessments that involve reading and writing

content area: the part of the curriculum that encompasses Math, Science, and Social Studies

cueing system: the sources of information that students use as they build meaning from print, including graphophonic (visual information), syntactic (language structures), and semantic (meaning) cues

decode: to analyze sound/symbol relationships to ascertain their intended meaning

demonstrate: to model or show someone else how to do something

diagram: a graphic organizer enhanced with labels to help the reader identify or define specific parts

directionality: the left-to-right movement across text

fluency: freedom from word-identification problems that might hinder comprehension in silent reading or the expression of ideas in oral reading

genre: different types of literary writing such as fiction, poetry, nonfiction, folktale, etc.

glossary: an alphabetical list in the back of a book that gives definitions of words in the book that may be unfamiliar to readers

graphic organizer: a visual representation that organizes information

graphs: graphic organizers for charting comparisons, such as bar graphs, column graphs, line graphs, and circle graphs

guided reading: see small-group reading

heading: a bold headline within the text, sometimes in the form of a summarizing question, intended to add purpose to the reading and to help the reader organize the content information

high-frequency words: the words students encounter most often in texts

index: an alphabetical list in the back of a book that tells the readers on which pages they can read to find information about topics and/or ideas in the book

integrated instruction: the process of overlapping curriculum areas throughout the school day

interactive writing: a collaborative assisted-writing activity that helps emergent and early writers acquire important writing concepts

label: a descriptive word used on an illustration or photograph to help the reader identify or define specific parts

labeled drawing: a combination of words and an illustration that promotes meaning by noting and naming component parts

language pattern: any words or grouping of words that are repeated within a text

language prompts: questions that stimulate students' problem-solving processes across a wide range of literacy activities

literacy centers: the areas in the classroom for small-group or independent practice that focus on reading and writing

map: a visual design with words and symbols that depicts place and location

mini-lesson: a brief, explicit lesson designed to help students learn literacy skills and become strategic independent readers and writers

modeling: a clear demonstration by the teacher, using explicit language

nonfiction: the literary genre that informs through photos, realistic drawings, and actual facts

one-to-one matching: voice-to-print match

oral reading record: a form of miscue analysis in which the teacher observes, records, and completes four levels of analysis on any unexpected words or substitutions that a student renders while reading

phoneme: the smallest unit of sound in spoken words that is represented by single letters or pairs of letters

phonemic awareness: the ability to analyze spoken words into phonemes

phonics: the relationship of phonemes (sounds) and graphemes (letters)

photograph: a real pictorial representation designed to support and enhance the content of the text

predictable text: a text that has been written with enough support that the reader can infer what words come next

prompts: see language prompts

reading behaviors: the observable characteristics that teachers can note as students are reading in order to gain a better understanding of how they are processing text

return sweep: the top-to-bottom return of the reader's eye from the end of a line of text (right) to the beginning of the next line (left)

scaffold: a support system for helping students achieve success on a task that would be too difficult for them to accomplish on their own

shared reading: a collaborative reading experience in which the teacher and the students join in reading together

small-group reading: an assisted literacy experience in which the teacher supports and guides a small group of students with similar strengths and needs on texts at their instructional level

sorts: the process of classifying letters or words into categories

sound/symbol relationship: the relationship of the phonemes (sounds) and graphemes (letters) in words

steps in a process: a sequence of events in the text that a reader uses to conduct an experiment

strategies: mental problem-solving actions initiated by the reader to gain meaning from the text

structured routines: organized instructional activities in the classroom setting that enable students to reach higher levels of literacy development

supportive text features: the aspects of the text that aid students as they read

table: an organized listing of information using words or numbers that is usually in rows or columns

table of contents: a graphic organizer found on the title page of each text that outlines the contents of the book

teaching points: the mini-lessons within a shared or guided reading lesson that help students apply problem-solving strategies

text levels: the gradient scale of difficulty that separates text by features or characteristics

text-dependent comprehension: a model in which students must "prove" their answers to comprehension questions based on direct statements or clues and evidence in the text

time line: a graphic organizer that places events within a chronological sequence

transfer: a student's ability to use existing knowledge of skills and strategies flexibly in all types of texts and for varying purposes

Bibliography

Adams, M. *Beginning to Read: Thinking and Learning About Print*. 9th ed. MIT Press, 1996.

Adams, M. J., B. Foorman, I. Lundberg, and T. Beeler. *Phonemic Awareness in Young Children*. Brookes Publishing Company, 1998.

Allen, J. *Words, Words, Words*. Stenhouse, 1999.

Allen, J. *Yellow Brick Roads: Shared and Guided Paths to Independent Reading 4–12*. Stenhouse, 2000.

Anderson, C. *How's It Going? A Practical Guide to Conferring With Students*. Heinemann, 2000.

Armbruster, B. B., F. Lehr, and J. Osborne. *Put Reading First: The Research Building Blocks for Teaching Children to Read*. National Reading Panel, National Institute for Literacy, the National Institute of Child Health and Human Development, and the U.S. Department of Education.

Atwell, N. *In the Middle: Writing, Reading, and Learning with Adolescents*. Heinemann, 1987.

Barrentine, S., ed. *Reading Assessment: Principles and Practices for Elementary Teachers*. International Reading Association, 1999.

Bear, D., M. Invernizzi, S. Templeton, and F. Johnston. *Words Their Way: Word Study for Phonics, Vocabulary, and Spelling Instruction*. Prentice-Hall, Inc., 1996.

Beaver, J. *Developmental Reading Assessment*. Celebration Press, 1997.

Beaver, T. *The Author's Profile: Assessing Writing in Context*. Stenhouse, 1998.

Belanoff, P., and M. Dickson, eds. *Portfolios: Process and Product*. Heinemann, 1991.

Blevins, W. *Phonemic Awareness Activities for Early Reading Success*. Scholastic, 1997.

Blevins, W. *Phonics from A to Z: A Practical Guide*. Scholastic, 1998.

Bodrova, E., and D. Leong. *Goals of the Mind: The Vygotskian Approach to Early Childhood*. Merrill, 1996.

Booth, D. *Guiding the Reading Process: Techniques and Strategies for Successful Instruction in K–8 Classrooms*. Stenhouse, 1998.

Booth, D., ed. *Literacy Techniques for Building Successful Readers and Writers*. Stenhouse, 1996.

Bromley, K., L. Irwin-De Vitis, and M. Modlo. *Graphic Organizers*. Scholastic, 1995.

Button, K., M. Johnson, and P. Furgerson. *"Interactive Writing in a Primary Classroom."* The Reading Teacher 49, no. 6 (1996): 446–454.

Caine, R. N., and G. Caine. *Making Connections: Teaching and the Human Brain*. Addison-Wesley, 1994.

Calkins, L. *The Art of Teaching Writing*. Heinemann, 1994.

Cardellichio, T., and W. Field. *"Seven Strategies That Encourage Neural Branching."* Educational Leadership 54, no. 6 (1997).

Carroll, J., and E. Wilson. *Acts of Teaching: How to Teach Writing*. Teacher Ideas Press, 1993.

Chambers, A. *Tell Me: Children, Reading, and Talk*. Stenhouse, 1996.

Clay, M. *Becoming Literate: The Construction of Inner Control*. Heinemann, 1991.

Clay, M. *An Observation Survey of Early Literacy Achievement*. Heinemann, 1993.

Clay, M. *Reading Recovery: A Guidebook for Teachers in Training*. Heinemann, 1993.

Cochran-Smith, M. *The Making of a Reader*. Ablex, 1989.

Collins, A., J. Brown, and S. Newman. *"Cognitive Apprenticeship: Teaching the Crafts of Reading, Writing, and Mathematics."* Knowing, Learning, and Instruction: Essays in Honor of Robert Glasser. L. Resnick, ed. Lawrence Erlbaum, 1989.

Cunningham, P. *Phonics They Use: Words for Reading and Writing*. 3rd ed. Addison Wesley Longman, 2000.

Cunningham, P., and R. Allington. *Classrooms That Work: They Can All Read and Write*. 2nd ed. Longman, 1996.

Dorn, L., C. French, and T. Jones. *Apprenticeship in Literacy: Transitions Across Reading and Writing*. Stenhouse, 1998.

Durrell, D. *Phonograms in Primary Grade Words*. Boston University, 1963.

Duthie, C. *True Stories: Nonfiction Literacy in the Primary Classroom*. Stenhouse, 1996.

Fiderer, A. *Practical Assessments for Literature-Based Reading Classrooms*. Scholastic, 1995.

Finch, F., ed. *Educational Performance Assessment*. Riverside, 1991.

Fisher, B. *Joyful Learning*. Heinemann, 1991.

Fletcher, R., and J. Portalupi. *Craft Lessons: Teaching Writing K–8*. Stenhouse, 1998.

Fletcher, R., and J. Portalupi. *Nonfiction Craft Lessons: Teaching Information Writing K–8*. Stenhouse, 2001.

Fletcher, R., and J. Portalupi. *Writing Workshop: The Essential Guide*. Heinemann, 2001.

Fogarty, R. *The Mindful School: Teach for Metacognitive Reflection*. IRI/Skylight Training and Publishing, Inc., 1994.

Foorman, B. R., D. J. Francis, J. M. Fletcher, C. Schatsschneider, and P. Mehta. *"The role of instruction in learning to read: Preventing reading failure in at-risk children."* Journal of Educational Psychology 90 (1998): 1–15.

Fountas, I., and G. S. Pinnell. *Guided Readers and Writers Grades 3–6: Teaching Comprehension, Genre, and Content Literacy*. Heinemann, 2002.

Fountas, I., and G. S. Pinnell. *Guided Reading: Good First Teaching for All Children*. Heinemann, 1996.

Fountas, I., and G. S. Pinnell. *Matching Books to Readers*. Heinemann, 1998.

Fountas, I., and G. S. Pinnell, eds. *Voices on Word Matters: Learning About Phonics and Spelling in the Literacy Classroom*. Heinemann, 1999.

Fountas, I., and G. S. Pinnell. *Word Matters! Teaching Phonics and Spelling in the Reading/Writing Classroom*. Heinemann, 1998.

Freeman, Marcia S. *Building a Writing Community*. Maupin House, 1995.

Freeman, Marcia S. *Teaching the Youngest Writers*. Maupin House, 1998.

Fry, E., J. Kress, and D. L. Fountoukidis. *The Reading Teacher's Book of Lists*. 3rd ed. Prentice Hall, 1993.

Gentry, J. R. *The Literacy Map: Guiding Children to Where They Need to Be K–3*. Mondo, 2000.

Gentry, J. R. *My Kid Can't Spell: Understanding and Assisting Your Child's Literacy Development*. Heinemann, 1997.

Gentry, J. R., and J. Gillet. *Teaching Kids to Spell*. Heinemann, 1993.

Gillet, J. W., and C. Temple. *Understanding Reading Problems: Assessment and Instruction*. HarperCollins, 1994.

Glazer, S. M. *Assessment Is Instruction: Reading, Writing, Spelling, and Phonics for All Learners*. Christopher-Gordon, 1998.

Glazer, S. M., and C. S. Brown. Portfolios and Beyond: Collaborative Assessment in Reading and Writing. Christopher-Gordon, 1993.

Graves, D. *Writing: Teachers and Children at Work*. Heinemann, 1983.

Harp, B. *The Handbook of Literacy Assessment and Evaluation*. Christopher-Gordon, 1996.

Harvey, S. *Nonfiction Matters: Reading, Writing, and Research in Grades 3–8*. Stenhouse, 1998.

Harvey, S., and A. Goudvis. *Strategies That Work: Teaching Comprehension to Enhance Understanding*. Stenhouse, 2000.

Hibbard, K. M., et al. *A Teacher's Guide to Performance-Based Learning and Assessment*. Association for Supervision and Curriculum Development, 1996.

Hill, B., and C. Ruptic. *Practical Aspects of Authentic Assessment: Putting the Pieces Together*. Christopher-Gordon, 1994.

Hill, B., C. Ruptic, and L. Norwick. *Classroom-Based Assessment*. Christopher-Gordon, 1998.

Hindley, J. *In the Company of Children*. Stenhouse, 1996.

Holdaway, D. *Foundations of Literacy*. Ashton Scholastic, 1979.

Hoyt, Linda. *Revisit, Reflect, Retell*. Heinemann, 1999.

Ingraham, P. *Creating and Managing Learning Centers: A Thematic Approach*. Crystal Spring Books, 1997.

Johnson, M. *Never Too Early to Write*. Maupin House, 1999.

Johnston, P. *Knowing Literacy: Constructive Literacy Assessment*. Stenhouse, 1997.

Juel, C. *"Beginning Reading."* Handbook of Reading Research 2 (1991).

Juel, C. *"Learning to read and write: A longitudinal study of 54 children from first through fourth grades."* Journal of Educational Psychology 80, no. 4 (1998): 437–447.

Juel, C., P. L. Griffith, and P. B. Gough. *"Acquisition of literacy: A longitudinal study of children in first and second grade."* Journal of Educational Psychology 78 (1986): 243–255.

Keene, E., and S. Zimmerman. *Mosaic of Thought: Teaching Comprehension in Reader's Workshop*. Heinemann, 1999.

Kohn, A. *The Schools Our Children Deserve: Moving Beyond Traditional Classrooms and "Tougher Standards."* Houghton Mifflin, 1999.

Learning First Alliance. *Every Child Reading: An action plan of the Learning First Alliance*. Washington, D.C., 1998.

Lundberg, I., A. Olofsson, and S. Wall. *"Reading and spelling skills in the first school years, predicted from phonemic awareness skills in kindergarten."* Scandinavian Journal of Psychology 21 (1980): 159–73.

Marzano, R., D. Pickering, and J. McTighe. *Assessing Student Outcomes*. Association for Supervision and Curriculum Development, 1993.

Moats, L. C. *"Teaching decoding."* American Educator Spring/Summer (1998): 42–49.

Moline, S. *I See What You Mean: Children at Work with Visual Information*. Stenhouse, 1995.

Moore, D., S. Moore, P. Cunningham, and J. Cunningham. *Developing Readers and Writers in the Content Areas K–12*. 3rd ed. Longman, 1998.

Morrow, L. *The Literacy Center: Contents for Reading and Writing*. Stenhouse, 1997.

Moustafa, M. *Beyond Traditional Phonics: Research Discoveries and Reading Instruction*. Heinemann, 1997.

National Center on Education and the Economy. *Reading and Writing Grade by Grade: Primary Literacy Standards*. Smith Lithograph Corporation, 1999.

National Institute of Child Health and Human Development. *Teaching Children to Read: An Evidence-Based Assessment of the Scientific Research Literature on Reading and Its Implications for Reading Instruction*. Report of the National Reading Panel, 2000.

Opitz, M., T. Rasinski, and L. Bird. *Good-Bye Round Robin: Twenty-Five Effective Oral Reading Strategies*. Heinemann, 1998.

Parkes, B. *Something Old, Something New: An Integrated Approach to Traditional Tales*. Rigby Education, 1993.

Perrone, V. *Expanding Student Assessment*. Association for Supervision and Curriculum Development, 1991.

Phenix, J. *Teaching Writing: The Nuts and Bolts of Running a Day-to-Day Writing Program*. Pembroke Publishers Limited, 1990.

Pinnell, G. S., and A. McCarrier. *"Interactive Writing: A Transition Tool for Assisting Children in Learning to Read and Write."* Getting Reading Right from the Start: Effective Early Literacy Interventions. Allyn and Bacon, 1994.

Popham, W. J. *Classroom Assessment: What Teachers Need to Know*. Allyn and Bacon, 1995.

Power, B. *Taking Note: Improving Your Observational Notetaking*. Stenhouse, 1996.

Rhodes, L., and N. Shanklin. *Windows Into Literacy: Assessing Learners K–8*. Heinemann, 1993.

Robb, L. *Easy to Manage Reading and Writing Conferences*. Scholastic, 1998.

Rogoff, B. *Apprenticeship in Thinking: Cognitive Development in Social Contexts*. Oxford University Press, 1990.

Routman, R. Conversations. Heinemann, 2000.

Routman, R. *Invitations: Changing as Teachers and Learners*. Heinemann, 1991.

Smith, F. *Understanding Reading*. Lawrence Erlbaum, 1994.

Snow, C., W. Barnes, J. Chandler, I. Goodman, and L. Hemphill. *Unfilled Expectations: Home and School Influences on Literacy*. Harvard University Press, 1991.

Snow, C .F., M. S. Burns, and P. Griffin. *Preventing Reading Difficulties in Young Children*. National Research Council and National Academy Press, 1998.

Sobel, D. *Mapmaking with Children: Sense of Place Education for the Elementary Years*. Heinemann, 1998.

Sousa, D. How the Brain Learns. National Association of Secondary Principals, 1995.

Stahl, S. *"Saying the 'P' Word: Nine Guidelines for Exemplary Phonics Instruction."* The Reading Teacher 45, no. 8 (1992).

Stahl, S. *"Teaching Children with Reading Problems to Recognize Words."* Readings on Language & Literacy: Essays in Honor of Jeanne S. Chall. Brookline Books, 1997.

Stiggins, R. J. *Student-Centered Classroom Assessment*. Macmillan, 1994.

Tharp, R., and R. Gallimore. *Rousing Minds to Life: Teaching, Learning, and School in Social Context*. Cambridge University Press, 1988.

Tierney, R., M. Carter, and L. Desai. *Portfolio Assessment in the Reading-Writing Classroom*. Christopher-Gordon, 1991.

Tovani, C. *I Read It, But I Don't Get It: Comprehension Strategies for Adolescent Readers*. Stenhouse, 2000.

Trelease, Jim. *The New Read-Aloud Handbook*. Penguin Books, 1989.

Tunmer, W. E., and A. R. Nesdale. *"Phonemic segmentation skill and beginning reading."* Journal of Educational Psychology 77 (1985): 417–427.

Vacca, R., and J. Vacca. *Content Area Reading: Literacy and Learning Across the Curriculum*. Longman, 1999.

Valencia, S., E. H. Hiebert, and P. Afflerbach. *Authentic Reading Assessment: Practices and Possibilities. International Reading Association*, 1994.

Vygotsky, L. *Mind in Society*. Harvard University Press, 1978.

Waterland, L. *Read with Me: An Apprenticeship Approach to Reading*. Thimble Press, 1985.

Wells, G., and G. Chang-Wells. *Constructing Knowledge Together*. Heinemann, 1992.

Wertsch, J. V. *Culture, Communication, and Cognition: Vygotskian Perspectives*. Cambridge University Press, 1985.

Wertsch, J. V. *"The Zone of Proximal Development: Some Conceptual Issues."* Children's Learning in the Zone of Proximal Development. Jossey-Bass, 1984.

Wiggins, G. *Assessing Student Performance*. Jossey-Bass, 1993.

Wiggins, G. *Educative Assessment: Designing Assessment to Inform and Improve Student Performance*. Jossey-Bass, 1998.

Wilhelm, J., Ph.D. *Improving Comprehension Through Think-Aloud Strategies*. Scholastic, 2001.

Wood, D. *How Children Think and Learn*. Basil Blackwell, 1988.

Wood, D. *"Teaching the Young Child: Some Relationships Between Social Interaction, Language, and Thought."* The Social Foundations of Language and Thought. W. W. Norton, 1980.

Zemelman, S., H. Daniels, and A. Hyde. *Best Practices: New Standards for Teaching and Learning in American Schools*. Heinemann, 1998.